THE MONKEY TREE

MICHELE HEENEY

THE

MONKEY

TREE

BY
MICHELE HEENEY

ARPress

ILLUMINATING IDEAS,
EMPOWERING VOICES

ARPress
45 Dan Road Suite 5
Canton MA 02021
Hotline: 1(888) 821-0229
Fax: 1(508) 545-7580

Ordering Information:
Quantity sales. Special discounts are available on quantity purchases by corporations, associations, and others. For details, contact the publisher at the address above.

Printed in the United States of America.

ISBN-13:	Softcover	979-8-89330-442-8
	Hardcover	979-8-89330-444-2
	eBook	979-8-89330-443-5

Library of Congress Control Number: 2024901181

TABLE OF CONTENTS

THE POEMS

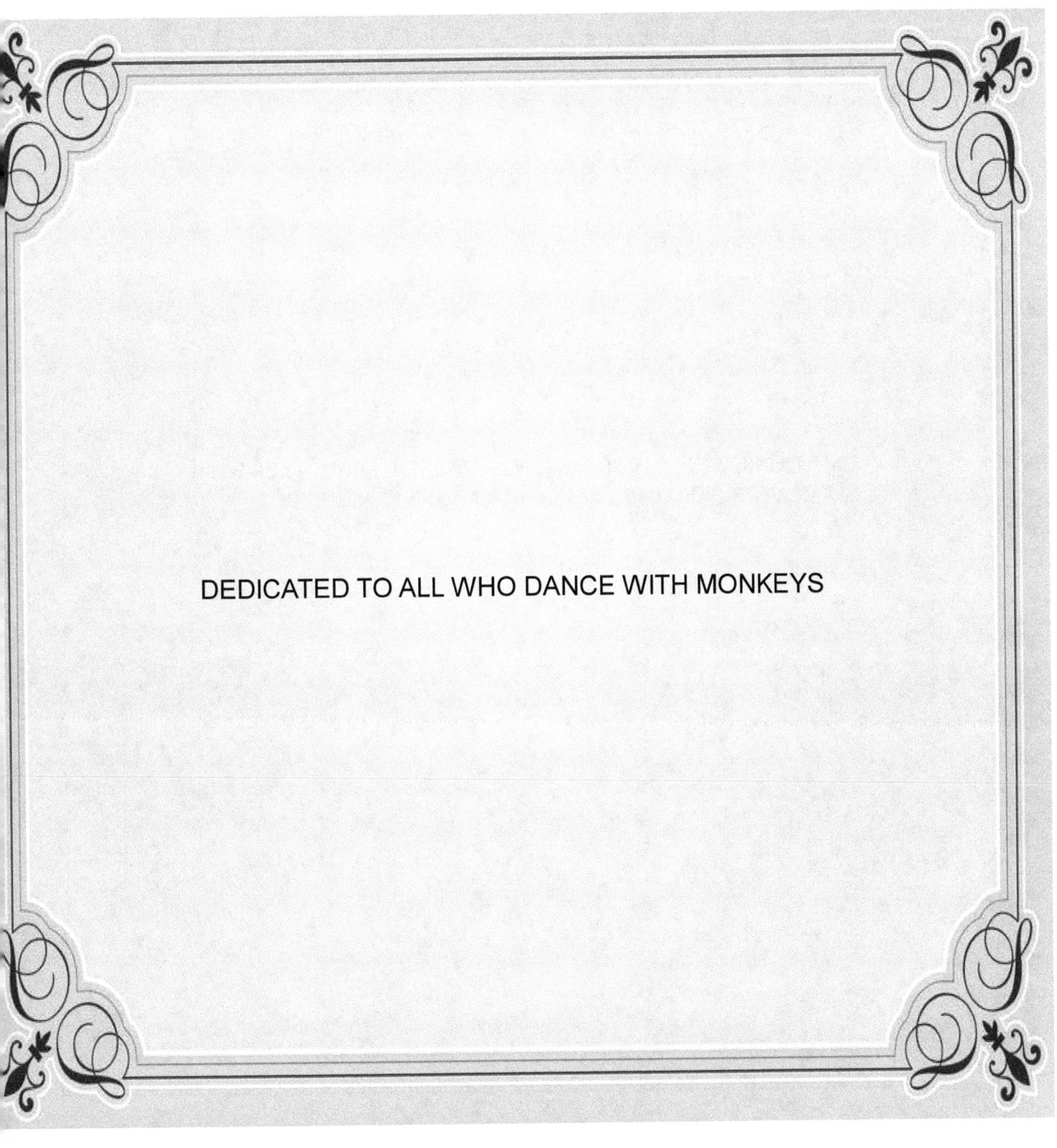

DEDICATED TO ALL WHO DANCE WITH MONKEYS

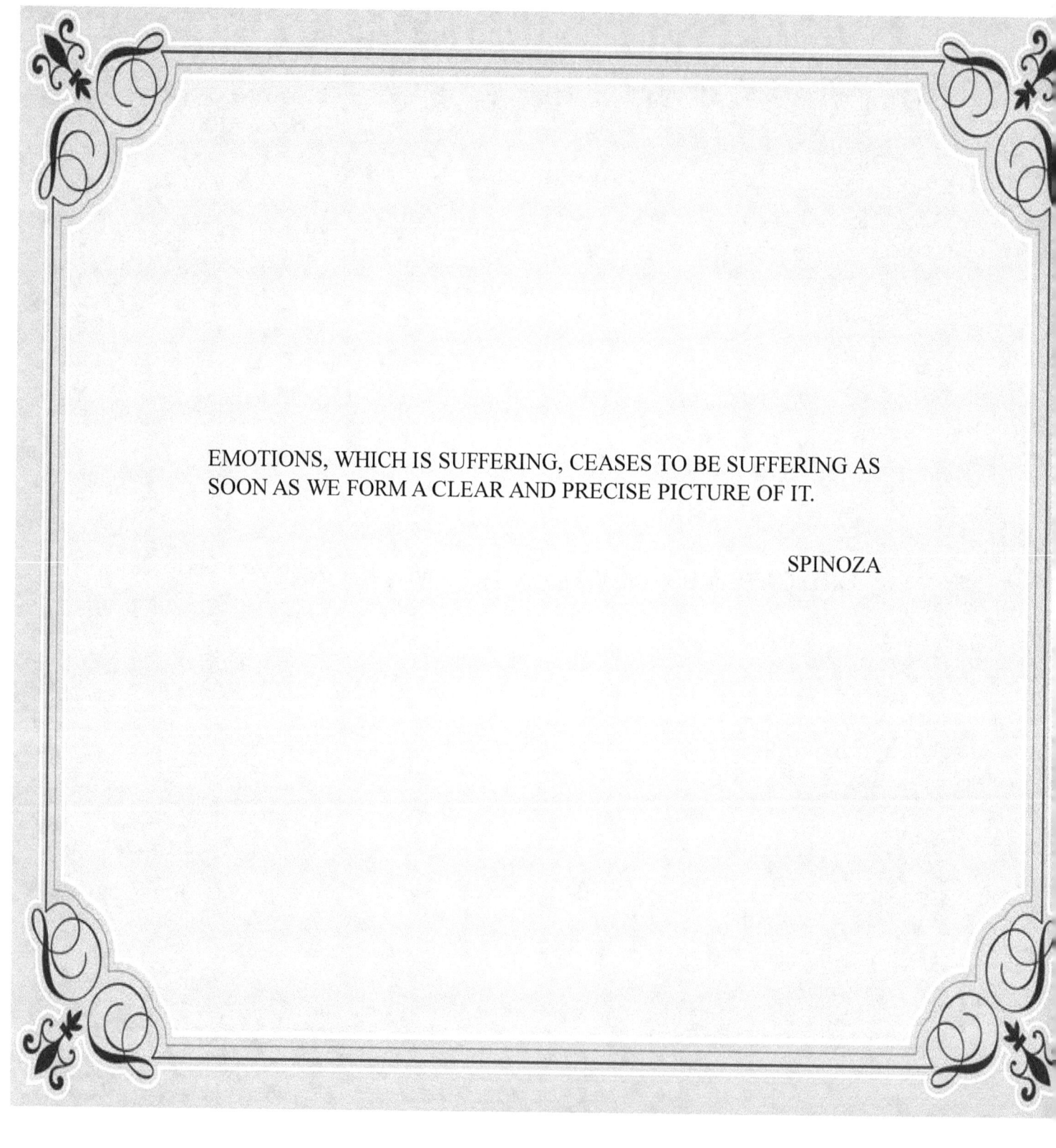

EMOTIONS, WHICH IS SUFFERING, CEASES TO BE SUFFERING AS
SOON AS WE FORM A CLEAR AND PRECISE PICTURE OF IT.

SPINOZA

The Poems

THE IMPOLITE, ALWAYS RIGHT MONKEY

Oh, no,
That monkey's
Back again.

Throws banana peels
At village matrons
And would be suitors.
Laughs loudly
In genteel company.
Corrects people's grammar
And long held beliefs.
Butts into private conversations.

I tell that monkey,
"Keep this up and
There will be
No birthday cards for us this year."

That monkey don't care,
Keeps on butting in.

Finally he's kaput.
Jumps off my back and
Out the window.

That crazy monkey.

TRANSITIONS

The small poet
Takes the fine pen
To probe delicate nerves
Of invisible emotion
Causing liquid tears
To evaporate
Into transparent air

And the whole world
Shifts.

TRAPPED

We are all
Born free.
Soon
Time comes
Stalking
The net drops
Down.

Tender flesh
Tender minds
Ensnared,
Sins
Recorded,
Runaways
Captured.

Trapped.

Trapped
Then thrown
To shadows.

And long before
We die
We are ghosts.

Grey ghosts
Condemned To
haunt

The few
Who got away.

NEW MEXICAN SKY

What calls us here?
Voices from the sky,

The majestic
Glittering
Night Sky

The dazzling
Sapphire
Day Sky

The Big Cosmic Mama
Pregnant with
The whole churning
Universe.

The voices of the ancients
Call us towards the sky.

Listen!
They call us still.

AFTER LOVE

My friend
Asked me
To her party.
I said I'd come
And bring
The cake.
She said, "No,
Bring forgiveness."

My parents
Asked me
To their grave.
I said I'd come
And bring
Red roses.
They said, "No,
Just bring forgiveness,"

The Holy Spirit
Whispered that
He had a gift
For me.
I opened it,
Sank to my knees
And wept.
It was forgiveness.

Surely, after Love,

Forgiveness is
The Golden Gift.

THE DANCE OF SHIVA

Eyebrows singed
Nose blistered and red
Lips cracked and scorched

My kinetic soul stood still
My body melted
Mind and thoughts burnt
Liked torched paper.

What happened !?

One tiny spark
Off the silver heels
Of the Eternal Dancer
Kissed me.

YOU'RE GOOD

What a talent!
You really
Are adept
Quite flawless,
Such dexterity.

With just
The slightest touch
Your knife
Hit solid bone--
Without a trace
Of blood.

WITH ME

With me
Just be.

No need
To lug around
Your suitcase
Full of crazy
Disguises.

With me
The pace
Is slow,
But rich
Like chocolate
And honey.

Pull up
Some music
Feel free
To jump in
And swim
With the words
And rhythm.

Judgement
Pretense
Guilt-
Leave them
At the door.

With me
Just be
No less
No more.

WHERE THE WILD THINGS ARE

We are delicate beings
Traversing the
Opulent space
In between
Immovable opposites.

The space in between
Darkness & light,
Earthbound & flight.

Between
Male & female,
Rudder & sail.

Between
Not knowing & knowing,
Taking & giving.

In that vast space
We may discover
Who we are,
And, if courageous,
One another.

MI BOLA DE ANNOS

My ball of years
Has grown
Quite large.
It shows how far
I've traveled.

It's frayed a bit
Around the edges
And often
Comes unraveled.

I do recall
When it
Was small,
About the size
Of a ping pong ball.

Now it's as Big
As the Moon
On an evening
In June.

The center's
Quite corroded

KABOOM

Dear Lord!
My ball of years
Has just exploded.

THE RUNNERS

I do grow weary with the ways of men,
The ways we have with each other.
How we speak, how we act, and then
How we tum our backs on our brother.

We live , yet we're dying
We see, yet we're blind
We take, but seldom think to give.
Learn, yet rarely know our minds.

Yet on we will go, as ever we went,
Racing in the wrong direction.
Why can't we run a gentler pace
To catch the sun s healing reflection?

BACK EAST

To the soft hills
Of my childhood
Where my parents lie,
Long years have they rested
Under Pennsylvania sky.

Back home,
No other thought
Holds such pain,
So far from my roots
I need a taste
Of home again.

Back to mountain winters,
To big oaks
And sprouting springs,
To the riot of autumn color
When the Allegheny sings.

Back home,
Though far too late,
With all my dear ones gone.
Alone and on my own,
It's well past time,
Past time,
That I go home.

TRAVEL GUIDE

Dublin
Stockholm
Alameda,

Paris
Lisbon
San Diego,

London
New York
Santiago,

Shannon
Boston
Montenegro,

Brussels
Rio
De Janeiro,

Roma
Sydney
San Cristobal,

Or on the continental shelf,

Where you go
Matters little
If you're not
Present in yourself.

CAR CRASH AHEAD

I only meant
To warn you
Of the potholes
In the road.

You quickly
Thought me
Quite the crank.

Yet you fail to witness
Large black leaks
In your existence.

A firm commitment
To avoid reality,
To insist on duality.

Drive on,
But if you crash and dent,
To me
Do not report
The accident.

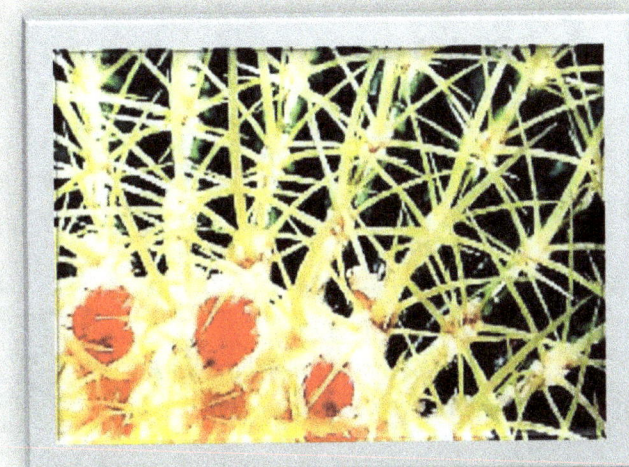

IN THE PICTURE

In the picture
A child sits
Under an oak tree.
A woman
In the house
Is staring out a window.
An angel comes
To tell the child
"She's sad and she's sick,
And it's not your fault."

Would you be
My angel
And whisper to me
"It's not your fault?"

FALLEN PETALS

I'm a special breed of rose.
Hold me too close
And I'll wither;
Not close enough
And I'll die.

POSSESSED

Dark heart,
Why do you live in darkness
While all around is light?

Why must you
Look at Sorrow
And take her
For your own?
Don't you see,
In wasting Beauty,
You've wasted Joy?

You create your Pain,
Then feed it daily.
Nurture it with care.

You build your life
With rotting wood,
When you see the rot,
You build all the more.

Now in that
Dark, strange place
You've made,
The Devil finds
His own.

STRANGE HOTEL

They both sit
Smoldering
In the depths
Of hell.

Eternal
Fight.

Each crouches
In the assigned corner,
Each thinking
"I am the saddest of souls,
The rare, consummate mourner."

One magic day
The gates opened wide,
(Though their misery
Is deep and abiding).
She refused freedom,
He chose hell.
They went deeper still
Into hiding.

Sadly, they live
In this strange hotel,
Bereft of joy
Or heavenly light.
Instead of sweet peace
They are passionately
Committed
To their demonic,

THE BUDDIST REQUEST

Boundless compassion?
I'm still busy
Climbing
The slippery
Slimy
Tree
Of Self

Growing out of
The soupy
Swamp
Of Samsara.

Boundless Compassion?
The very minute
I get out of
This damn tree.

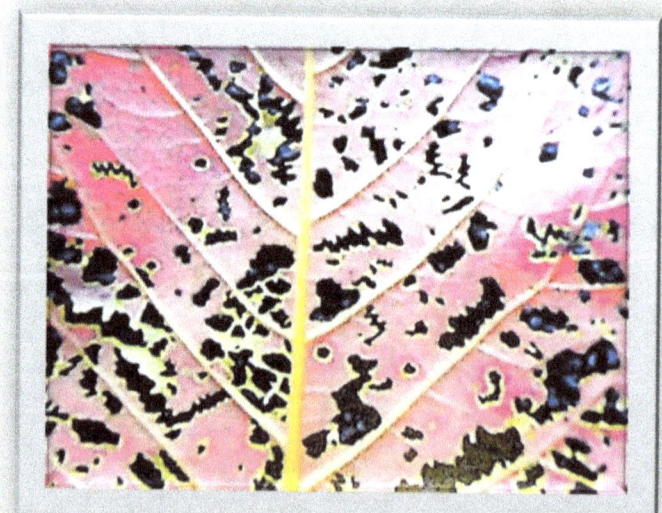

FROM NOON TO MORNING

We sailed softly through
The black satin sky,
On towards the lemon moon.
Off starboard, galaxies floated by
As we sang our sailor's tune.

By magenta morning
You were gone from me,
Slipped off into the night,
Now I wander alone on
This star-filled sea,
Adrift on this astral flight.

Sometimes I can just
Catch sight of you
While you skim
The face of the sun.

I doubt we'll sail together again,
As I steer my ship of one,
Compass in hand,
Wind at my back,
I steer my ship of one.

THE KNIFE

Of all the cuts into my heart,
And there have been many,
Yours went the deepest
By far, than any.

THE YEAR OF THE HORSE

My year with you was like
Riding a greased horse
Whose tail was soaked in oil
Braided with sticks of dynamite,
Each leg, a different length.

Loving you was
Riding this horse
Up a slippery hill
Into an ice storm
With no saddle,
No bit between his teeth.

Then, one spark too many,
We both exploded
Into shiny pieces and bits
(Much like the stars)
Across the night sky.

MY HORSE, CUERPO

This good old horse,
Been riding her
All my life.

We've galloped
In and out
Of a thousand
Wild adventures.

Been half way
Round the world
And back again.

We sure have seen
A lot of trouble,
Seen a lot of Joy.

Knees getting bad,
Shoulders worn away,
Still, she gets around some.

I guess I'll ride
This old mare
To the end of the trail.

Old and tired,
She is My Own,
She'll get us home.

A LITTLE SHALLOW

Cerebral
Is fine
But handsome
Does it
Every time.

DELICATE MEASURES

Ski down
  The endless
    Mountainside
      Of time,
        Ecstasy flies.

Contemplate
  The boundless
    Scattering
      Of stars,
        Humility dawns.

Sail
  The infinite
    Ocean of
      Human love,
        Hearts break open.

Glimpse
  Humanity's
    Exquisite Sorrows,
      Senses are stunned.

Weighed on
  Intricate scales
    Of wisdom,
      Notions of duality
        Measure even.

AT ESALEN
For Sogyal Rinpoche

If your teacher
Begins to
Expand into
Rays of light

If the light
Begins to
Shimmer into
Clear bright color

If your body
Melts
And pain evaporates

If everything but
Luminosity
Falls away

You've just
Been hit
With the spirit
Of Dzogchen.

CHRISTMAS

Christmas comes but once a year.

I think that's rather nice,

Because the good lord only knows

I couldn't take it twice.

THE DIG

There's a mud hole
In my mind,
A rich, archeological dig.

I muck about and
Come up with
All sorts of artifacts.

They're in there.
I just need some
High waders
And a shovel
For digging up
Old bones.

Words, lost feelings,
Forgotten memories,
Good reasons
For bad behavior,
Amazing finds.

Dutifully, I write
Record, classify.

Just one thing-
That mud hole is
Most productive
At three o'clock
In the morning.

THE MEAN GREEN MONKEY

That monkey's
Back again.

Lobs obscenities at officials,
Drastically diagnoses
The mildly deranged,
Curses good Christian folk,
Frowns at and frustrates friends.

I tell that monkey
"Keep this up
And we are destined
For severe social sanctions."

That monkey don't care,
Keeps on scowling.

Finally, he's kaput.
Jumps off my back
And out the window.

That crazy monkey!

GOING DOWN SLOW

Coming back
To where
I started,
I realize
Why I left.

This plush
Velvet prison,
This sea
Of bland tranquility
Where all the rules
Are set.

I'm going down slow,
In this bog
Of conventionality,
This subtle brutality.

With not a soul
To save me.

MISS BOO CAT

The cat left.

I grieved
I cried
I nearly died.

I loved her so.

Two months went by,
She never showed
More tears flowed.

I felt so sad
Life seemed so weird,
Until the day
She reappeared.

TO AN OLD LOVE

Oh what a masquerade
I played
To please you.

You left anyway.

I simply could
Have been myself,
Then, at least
You would
Be leaving
Me.

SEVERELY ANEMIC

Your conversation is
Verbal cotton candy:
Sticky, pink and fluffy,
Dissolving into nothing
In my mouth.

Chewing on sweet air,
Gagging on
Spun sugar,

Tell me
Something real,
Something brief and witty,
A few nuggets of wisdom,
A morsel of truth,

It needn't be
Grade A,
But after talking with you
I feel the need
To tear into
A big chunk of
Red, raw meat.

HOW TO MAKE PESTO

Pesto, wonderful pesto,
On pasta,
Pesto pasta.
Oh, the taste.
Fresh green dynamite
On your tongue.

There's nothing
Quite like pesto.
Take basil, parmesan,
Garlic, olive oil and
Blendo, (ah, the fragrance)
Then, presto-
Pesto!

THE SCHEMING DREAMING MONKEY

That monkey's back again.

Lazing through fine autumn days,
Dreaming of wild adventures
In tropical countries,
Longing for equatorial flora,
Scheming of ways to blow this town.

I tell that monkey,
"Keep this up
And we'll miss out on
The sweet juice
Of today."

That monkey don't care,
Keeps on dreaming.

Finally, he's kaput.
Jumps off my back
And out the window.

That crazy monkey!

RESPITE

Step lightly.
Whisper.
Don't wake
My muse.

She'll be back
Soon enough,
A screaming banshee
Thrashing through
My brain,
Tearing up
The night,
And Oh,
The days!

So, at least,
Until tomorrow—

Tiptoe.

PSYCHOSANGUINOUS

You refused
To love me.
My heart
Ripped open.

Now, each time
I think of you
My heart
Bleeds.

You see!
Just now,
This blood
Dripping
On
The
Floor
     *
        *
          *

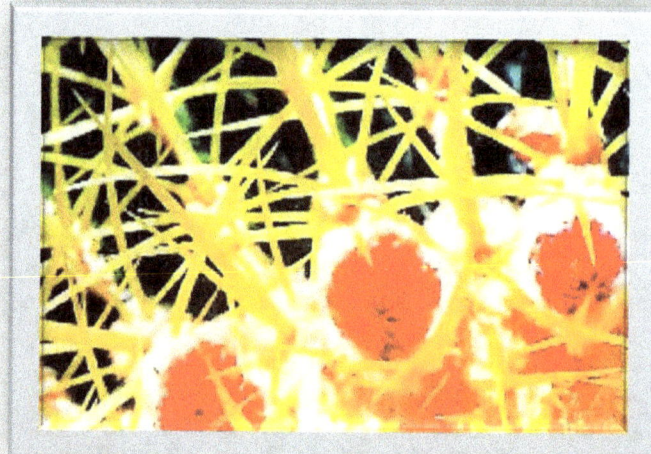

WRONG, BOX

Please don't put me
In your box.
It's not my box.
It's much too small.
My spirit's grown
To ten feet tall.
I won't fit in
A box at all.

If you feel you must
Rename me,
Label and contain me,
Then wrap me in a bag with
rocks,
Drop me in the deepest river,
Or put me in a cell that locks,
But please, and now I'm begging,
Don't put me
In a box.

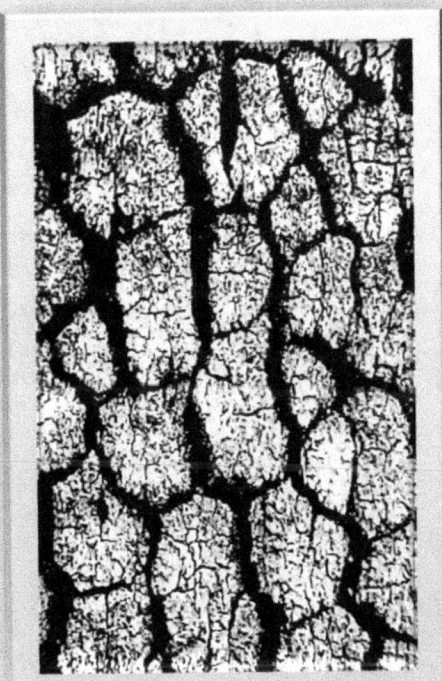

NO CHANCE

You are so firmly planted
In a world of force and logic,
Can you dare imagine
A translucent, subtle world
Of flow and light?

I find no way
To break you open
To the luminous
That so easily
Exists for me.

No chance
Of our worlds colliding.
We're not circling
The same sun.

TEA CUP

You dropped us
Onto the tile floor,
We shattered
Into a thousand
Tiny slivers.
You never came back
To sweep them up--
These jagged pieces
Of our fine
China teacup.

GENOME SOUP

I've read a book on genetics
That helped me clearly see,
I'm nothing more or nothing less
Than a souped up chimpanzee.

I've secretly suspected
Something like that,
A baboon, a monkey
Or Orangutan, Sassy, orange and fat.

This may startle you still further,
Put you in hysteria,
But before the chimp,
I'm kin to some old bacteria.

Don't go all snobby on me
Or act like you always knew
That my origins were iffy,
The same facts apply to you.

SHIVA

Look to the sky-
No beginning
No end.

Beyond the edge
Of the universe,
My home,
No borders
No boundaries
Only infinity.

For me
Time Is
A circle-
No first...
No last...
But always.

I was
Before eternity...
I will be
After eternity.

Contemplating
Space and time
Brings you closer
To me.

Come closer.

CALLING

Over here,
This small voice
Calling from a corner
Of the universe.

Over here,
Come find me.
I have a world of wondrous
Jewels in my pocket.

Come find me
And I'll share
Them all,
One by
Wondrous one,
With you.

ART, SCIENCE AND GEOGRAPHY

We humans
Are hot cauldrons
Of art and science.

We spill over,
Pour out,
Erupt.

Miniature Kilaueas
Spewing forth
Raw, new land
Into infinity.

NEW MEXICO DREAM

Raw, west winds
Sweep across
Wide mesas.
Exquisite sky,
The canopy.

Willful spirits
Rip through
Troops of Juniper.
Only the deeply rooted stand.

All else
Long, long since
Blown away.

To the pleasure
Of the desert gods,
Coyotes sing
Their crazy love song
To this fearsome Beauty.

Such is my interior canvas:
A wide, clean swept soulscape
In pale earth tones.

Yet, sometimes
In deepest sleep,
I dream of cool,
Moist nights,
Soft mists rising
Off verdant fields.

How could I not?
Celtic rain runs with
Ancient memories
Through my blood.

TRAVELING BAREFOOT

Traveling barefoot.
No map,
No hat
Against the searing sun.
Sheer will
To power me,
I've tripped forward
Into life.

Blinded by sweat,
Soaked through
From tremendous toil,
Roadless at times,
Half lost most days,
I ran straight into
Walls of stone.

Yet, battered and bruised,
] have found my way,
With the guidance of saints
And the luck of fools.

UNDER THE RUG

The Chuckawalla
Baby Bite Choo man
Lived under the living room rug.

He was absolutely terrifying,
Even though he was
The size of a bug.

He had long green teeth,
Blood red eyes,
And frequent raging fits.

One day the dog
Came galumphing by
And smashed him all to bits.

Apparently a paw
Came crashing down
And caught him in the neck.

Although it's been
A year since then,
His wife is still a wreck.

LA BEBIDA

When it comes to love
I often find
A small sip of poison
Is just as fine
As a big full glass
Of the best French wine.

I WAS

Baffled in Buffalo,
Sad in Sacramento,
Scared in Scranton,
Frantic in Fresno.

I was
Foolish in Philly,
Shocked in Chicago,
Miffed in Memphis,
Disgusted in D.C.

I was
Anxious in Austin,
Mired in Milwaukee,
Flummoxed in Florida,
Lost in Los Angeles...

Now I am
Nearly manic in New Mexico,
And on my way
To a brutal breakdown
In Brazil

MEXICO

Mexico, sweet Mexico,
Your sunsets glow
Your colors flow
Your warm winds blow.

Now all I want to do
Is go
To Mexico.

I hear the whisper
Of the brown Madonna's song
The music of fiestas wafts
along,
I love your high Sierra Madre,
Your salty sensual sea,

Please, Mexico,
Save a little place for me.

HARD SHELL ADVICE

As I was saying
To my cat
The other day,

If you're planning
Reincarnating,
I would not
Repeat, would not
Be resituating
Into any version
Of humanity.

If you must, however,
I'd steer
Well clear
Of anyone
Brandishing a loaded
Bible, Torah, or Quran.

This triad
Started badly
And they are sadly
still carping madly.

Some glitch about
Family ties
Or who gets the prize
Or some esoteric point.

No, Miss Boo Cat,
I'd go with turtles.

A FEW WORDS FROM THE MONKEY

Oh, No!
That small-minded
Silly human being.

SO committed to logic,
Married to all the rules.
Never dancing barefoot
In the rain.
Afraid of free flights
From tall trees
Into thin air.

I tell that human
"Keep this up
And we'll be having
No fun,
Nowhere."

That human don't care.
Keeps on sailing
The pale beige doldrums.

I'm outta here.

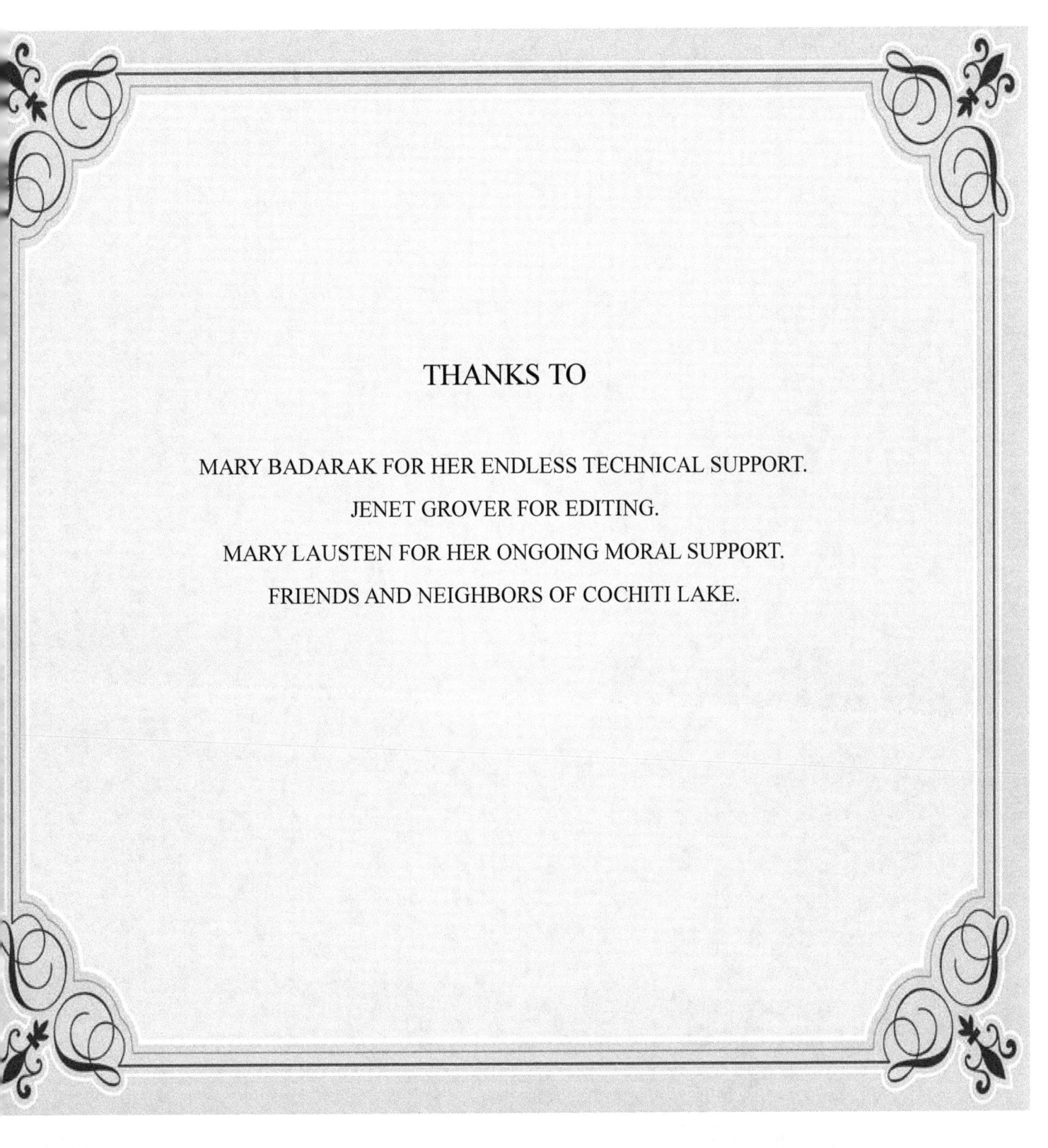

THANKS TO

MARY BADARAK FOR HER ENDLESS TECHNICAL SUPPORT.

JENET GROVER FOR EDITING.

MARY LAUSTEN FOR HER ONGOING MORAL SUPPORT.

FRIENDS AND NEIGHBORS OF COCHITI LAKE.